How To Cast Out Devils

How To Cast Out Devils

by
Norvel Hayes

HARRISON HOUSE
Tulsa, Oklahoma

Unless otherwise indicated,
all Scripture quotations are taken from
the *King James Version* of the Bible.

10th Printing

How To Cast Out Devils
ISBN 0-89274-706-4
Copyright © 1982 by Norvel Hayes
P. O. Box 1379
Cleveland, Tennessee 37311
(Formerly *Jesus Taught Me To Cast Out Devils*,
ISBN 0-89274-272-0)

Published by Harrison House, Inc.
P. O. Box 35035
Tulsa, Oklahoma 74153

Contents

Foreword

It is a pleasure for me to write a foreword to this book. When a person has a deep respect and protective inclination toward a person who is achieving his life's goal, he becomes spiritually involved with his progress. This is certainly my attitude toward Norvel Hayes. I have observed him very closely and rejoiced in every spiritual growth and victory of his life.

When I first met Norvel, I accepted him as a deacon of the First Baptist Church, a successful businessman, and a friend with a very pleasing personality.

However, after meeting him at one of my crusades in Tennessee and later at a Full Gospel Businessmen's rally and when he arrived at my revival crusade at the Orange Bowl in San Bernardino, California, I realized he was seeking something of me. He said the Lord told him to come and help me. I welcomed him and he assisted with the ushering and at the book table. At that moment, I did not realize that God was preparing him for an unusual ministry of divine deliverance and spiritual exorcism.

In the San Bernardino crusade, Norvel witnessed healings and deliverances from demon power. In that crusade, three people were brought from hospitals for the insane and he saw them relieved of demon oppression and set free.

One of these from the hospital broke away from her attendant and ran from the building before we could minister to her. I called to Norvel and Rev. James Murphy to catch the woman and bring her back. This they did. As they returned with her, I spoke from the platform and said, "Now cast that spirit of insanity out of her!" The Baptist deacon lost his composure. He was willing, but what would he say, and how would he do it? He repeated the words I called to them and demanded the spirit to release her and she was set free as the two prayed over her.

Since that time Norvel has visited us in South Bend many times to sit under our teaching and also minister to our people in return. He has been greatly appreciated and loved by the people.

Norvel Hayes is one of a new breed of laymen who has a deep desire to set humanity free. We know that this book will have a real impact upon those needing deliverance from demon power. Norvel believes the last words Jesus spoke on the face of this earth before going back to the Father, "And these signs shall follow them that believe; In my name shall they cast out devils . . . " (Mark 16:17). Jesus did not promise this just to His first disciples or apostles but to anyone who had faith. This faith is what makes Norvel Hayes an unusual person, desiring to set many free.

LESTER SUMRALL

1

A Woman Attacked Me in Church

Years ago, I was invited to visit the "Joe Pyne Show" in Hollywood, California, along with Dr. Lester Sumrall. Through that engagement that night with Joe Pyne in Hollywood, Joe Pyne was so impressed that he asked us to stay overnight in Hollywood and meet him the next morning. So, we did. And the next morning, when we met Joe Pyne, he asked us to go with him to his radio broadcast; and when it was all over, he thanked us very kindly and told us it had been a long time since he was so impressed with what he had heard.

After we left Joe Pyne, Dr. Lester Sumrall said to me, "I'm starting a crusade in San Bernardino, California, at the Orange Dome Auditorium tonight. I would certainly appreciate it if you would go to San Bernardino with me, and on this first great night of the crusade it would mean so much to the people to hear what Jesus means to a businessman. I would like for you to take at least fifteen minutes and give a testimony for Jesus and what He has done for you."

So I agreed to do it; and on the first night at San Bernardino I was introduced as a businessman, and I told those people some of the things that Jesus had done for me.

After I finished my testimony that night, Jesus was so kind to me, and He spoke very gently to me and said, "Don't leave yet."

That night after the service I went and told Dr. Sumrall

that Jesus had plainly told me not to leave yet, and Dr. Sumrall said to me, "Good."

And it was good, as it changed my entire life. However, I didn't think it was so good on the third day of the crusade—when a demon-possessed woman attacked me!

It was in the morning service, and God's power was moving strongly, and I was just sitting there in a seat next to the front with tears flowing down my cheeks, just being blessed by God's holy presence.

Towards the end of the service I got up, and a woman walked up to me. She didn't look like anything was wrong with her, but she said to me, "I believe that you are a man of God. Every time I come to town, there is something that causes real severe pains to begin to shoot through my shoulders and back. It is like something jumped on me, and I have to get my neighbor to come and get me and drive my car back home. This only happens to me when I come downtown, and I would like for you to pray for me."

The Spirit of the Lord had really been surging through me that morning, and I was feeling so good all through my body that I said to the lady, "Very well, I will pray for you. Just give me your hands and I will pray."

I reached my hands out, and she reached her hands out —and the moment our hands touched each other's, she jumped back two or three steps and shoved her fist up, and began to look at me straight in the eye. And she began to growl like a tiger and held her fist up in front of her face like she wanted to fight me.

Well, I never had a woman growl at me like this. I was raised in the Southern Baptist Church and I helped build the First Baptist Church, and we never had anybody that growled at anybody else up at the altar, so I didn't know what to do. But my mind began to whirl at a fast pace, and I began to think, "What's wrong with this crazy woman?"

I made up my mind real quick: I'm not going to let this crazy woman beat me up here in front of this congregation. Still, she kept me standing there looking at me with her fists up in the air, still growling like a tiger. I was so embarrassed I didn't know what to do.

In a few seconds she came plowing into me like a bull making a charge, and I reached out and grabbed one of her arms with force and held her away from me—and the moment I did that, her whole body began to quiver, and she quivered slowly down to the floor; just lying there, still quivering and making a funny noise.

Then I heard a strong voice coming through the air from Dr. Lester Sumrall, and he said, "Cast that thing out of her and don't let her speak."

As I said, I was a First Baptist boy; and in the First Baptist Church we didn't cast anything out of anybody. I didn't know what to do, but I didn't want the congregation to think that I was so stupid that I couldn't follow Dr. Sumrall's orders.

I had no idea that his orders were the same words Jesus spoke, and a command from Jesus for us to obey. I had never been attacked in church before. Nobody had ever taught me to cast anything anyplace—but today I thank God for Mr. Murphy.

Mr. Murphy is Dr. Sumrall's brother-in-law. He was standing close by me, and he walked over to the woman who was lying flat on her back on the floor quivering and making a funny noise, and he said, "In Jesus' name, come out of her."

Not knowing what to say, and not wanting the congregation to think I was stupid, I repeated after Mr. Murphy. I said, "Oh, sure . . . yes, come out."

Mr. Murphy was speaking with authority and he seemed to say it more strongly. He said, "Come out of her."

And then I repeated, "Oh, yes, I said it too. Come out." (To be honest about it, I didn't know what I was saying, much less what I was doing.))

It is amazing sometimes the position you get in with God, and how He can train you to know the truth. Mr. Murphy kept on saying "In Jesus' name, I command you to turn this woman loose and come out of her."

I didn't know what was in her, but I knew *something* was, and that it wasn't normal. And I had discovered by this time that we were talking to something else besides the woman, because he was telling something to come out of her. And it certainly was not ladylike to lie on the floor flat on your back, quivering and making funny noises.

Mr. Murphy would say, "I mean what I say: in Jesus' name, come out of her."

And I would just say, "I mean it too: yes, come on out now."

To my utter amazement, in about five minutes she just stopped quivering all of a sudden and a great peace came over her face and a great joy came to her and she began to cry with tears of joy. She began to rejoice. She began to thank Jesus, and she turned into one of the most beautiful ladies I saw in that meeting. We helped her get up, and she sat in a seat very quietly, with the joy of the Lord all over her and a great joy coming out of her.

She looked like an angel sitting there, with the peace of

God in her life—completely set free and the joy of the Lord flowing out of her. It seemed as though it were a river of living water, a continuous flow out of her. She looked like I had felt a few minutes before I started praying for her. Then I began to realize that the Devil wants to rob the human race of the joy of the Lord. Satan doesn't want your life to be full of God's joy. It was a beautiful experience for her.

This woman was a stranger to me, but now she looked like she had the joy of an angel. A few minutes before, she had attacked me. You see, the Spirit of the Lord had been blessing me, and the Devil was mad. The Devil knows that he can't have the blessings of God anymore—and it makes him mad if *you* enjoy God's blessings.

After that service, Jesus said to me, "You can go now."

So I left Dr. Sumrall and went down to Los Angeles, California, I had a friend whose office was in Los Angeles, and I walked into his office. His receptionist was a beautiful girl. I walked up in front of her desk and asked if my friend was in, and she said, "Just a few minutes and he will be with you—he is busy right now."

While I was standing there, just as soon as she opened her mouth and began to talk, my spirit became real grieved. Within my spirit I knew that the Devil had sent her there to wreck him. But how do you tell your friend who has a lovely wife that his secretary has been sent to him by the Devil to wreck him? My friend, you see, was a Christian. My friend loved Jesus. He was working for Jesus.

I stayed in a hotel in downtown Los Angeles that night, and I walked the floor for a long, long time that night, battling with God. God was trying to get me to go and tell my friend that his secretary had been sent to him by the Devil to destroy his marriage and to destroy his witness for Jesus and to wreck his home.

But I didn't give in to that mission—and later on, it happened just like the Lord had shown me: My friend's home was wrecked. He did get a divorce. I did go talk to him after his divorce, and I asked him if he knew for sure that Jesus was still with him—and he talked as though he did.

I heard later that they were going to get married—he and his secretary. But at that particular time in my life, I didn't know very much about the operation of the Devil, demons, and foul spirits, and the Devil would use any trick in the book to stop God's man.

The Devil is so deceiving. He knows the lonely spots and the empty spots in a man's life, and he will try to fill it up with something that is phony. And that is the very reason that we should study the writing of Paul in the New Testament, where he says, "Put on the whole armour of God, that you may be able to withstand the wiles of the Devil." (*See* Ephesians 6:11, 13.)

The Devil is here for three reasons, and they are to kill, to steal, and to destroy.

Please believe me: that means you and your house. The Devil has no respect for you or any member of your family, especially if you show any interest in God's Son, the Lord Jesus Christ—and Jesus is the only One who can give you real life that the world knows nothing about.

You might say, "What about me? I don't have this life of joy." Yet it's so simple—just ask Jesus to help you. Tell Him you are sorry for your sins and ask Him to come into your heart and life. And you want to know something? He *will* come in and lead you daily, if you will pray a lot and read the Bible—God's Word.

I left Los Angeles and flew back to Chattanooga, Tennessee, and went to my office in Cleveland, Tennessee, to catch up on my work. One day as I was riding in my car just after I returned to Tennessee, the Word of the Lord came unto me—and again Jesus plainly spoke to me —saying, "Son, I want you to study the last chapter of Mark."

I went and opened my Bible. I didn't even know what was in the last chapter of the Book of Mark. I turned quickly to the last chapter—the sixteenth chapter—and began to read the first verse. And it said, "And when the sabbath was past, Mary Magdalene. . . . "

I remembered that name. She was the woman that Jesus cast seven devils out of; and it was amazing how, when I read that name on that day, a great wave of penetrating love began to flow through my very being. But from what I felt that day it is doubtful that any human that lived loved Jesus more than Mary Magdalene did.

But the first verse says, "And when the sabbath was past, Mary Magdalene, and Mary the mother of James, and Salome, had bought sweet spices, that they might come and anoint him. And very early in the morning the first day of the week, they came unto the sepulchre at the rising of the sun. And they said among themselves, Who shall roll us away the stone from the door of the sepulchre? And when they looked, they saw that the stone was rolled away: for it was very great. And entering into the sepulchre, they saw a young man sitting at the right side, clothed in a long white garment; and they were affrighted. . . . "

2

Jesus Said to Me, "Go and Study the Sixteenth Chapter of Mark"

" . . . And he saith unto them, Be ye not affrighted: Ye seek Jesus of Nazareth, which was crucified: he is risen; he is not here: behold the place where they laid him. But go your way, tell his disciples and Peter that he goeth before you into Galilee: there shall ye see him, as he said unto you. And they went out quickly, and fled from the sepulchre; for they trembled and were amazed: neither said they any thing to any man; for they were afraid. Now when Jesus was risen early the first day of the week, he appeared first to Mary Magdalene. . . . "

And when I stopped on that day right here when Jesus told me to study this chapter and I came to this name in this verse, a great wave of God's love began to flow. Let me read verse 9 to you again: "Now when Jesus was risen early the first day of the week, *he appeared first to Mary Magdalene,* out of whom he had cast seven devils."

Let me stop here and talk to you for a minute. Isn't it strange that Jesus should appear to a woman who used to be possessed with devils before He would appear to anybody else? But, oh, the love that surged through me that day! And I know that Mary Magdalene loved Jesus with all her heart.

Verses 10 through 14 say, " . . . she went and told them that had been with him, as they mourned and wept. And they, when they had heard that he was alive, and had been seen of her, believed not. After that, he appeared in another form unto two of them, as they walked, and went into the country. And they went and told it unto the residue: neither believed they them. Afterward he appeared unto the eleven, as they sat at meat, and upbraided them with their unbelief and hardness of heart, because they believed not them which had seen him after he was risen."

On that day when I came to verse 15, the Word of the Lord came unto me, saying, "Now these are the most important words that ever came out of My mouth." And I thought to myself, oh my, they must be great then, to be the greatest words that Jesus ever spoke, And I began to read verse 15. It says, "And he said unto them [*he* meaning Jesus], Go ye into all the world, and preach the gospel to every creature."

Then I believed that there was nothing on earth for today any greater than the Gospel, because the Gospel is the Good News of the Lord Jesus Christ. The Gospel is the power of God unto Salvation, and verse 16 says—the words of Jesus say—"He that believeth and is baptized shall be saved; but he that believeth not shall be damned."

When I got to verse 17, the Word of the Lord came unto me, saying, "Hardly anyone on earth obeys verse 17 now. Most of them have quit, most of them have stopped through their unbelief."

Jesus makes a bold statement in verse 17—to me, and to you. He says, "And these signs shall follow them that believe; In my name shall they cast out devils. . . . "

Let me ask you, are you a believer? Let me ask you the next question that follows that. In Jesus' name, are you casting out devils? I wasn't and I didn't want to. In the

First Baptist Church, they had never taught me how to cast out devils; and when you are born and raised as a Baptist, you know what *they* know, but you don't know any more.

But now, here Jesus has got me studying the Bible, and He has brought me face to face with the Book of Mark. He has brought me face to face with the seventeenth verse of the sixteenth chapter of the Book of Mark, where He has made a bold statement, saying, "These signs shall follow them that believe; In my name shall they cast out devils. . . . "

I said, "Oh, Jesus, I didn't know I was supposed to. Forgive me." I remembered seeing that woman in California, how the Devil went out of her and how beautiful it was. "But, Jesus," I said, "I belong to the First Baptist Church—what are You showing *me* this for? They don't do that in there."

He plainly let me know that nearly everybody had quit, but He wanted to train me and He wanted me to obey the Scripture. And He plainly told me that although nearly everybody had quit, verse 17 chapter 16 of the Book of Mark is still true.

He said, "My Words, they never change. And, son, you have sense enough to read. You read and study that verse and you will see that is My first commission for any believer."

I said, "Jesus, I'm a believer; I believe in You."

He said, "Then I want you to show Me by fulfilling this verse of Scripture."

I said, "Jesus, I don't know how—but I ask You to show me, train me. I'm open to Your Word and what it says. And, Jesus, You know that I have been sick and tired a long time listening to what men say about Your Word. I want to know for myself."

The last part of verse 17 says, " . . . they shall speak with new tongues." And verse 18 adds, "They shall take up serpents; and if they drink any deadly thing, it shall not hurt them; they shall lay hands on the sick, and they shall recover."

The verses that follow—verses 19 and 20—conclude the chapter and the Book of Mark: "So then after the Lord had spoken unto them, he was received up into heaven, and sat on the right hand of God. And they went forth, and preached every where, the Lord working with them, and confirming the word with signs following."

I find that to be true today. Everywhere I go when I obey the Scripture, I see signs follow. If I don't obey the Scripture, then I don't see signs follow. But I made up my mind several years ago that I am going to start to obey God's Word instead of what men tell me and instead of what men think about the Bible. You see, it doesn't make any difference what you think about the Bible or what I think about the Bible; it is what the Bible actually says that is the only thing that makes any difference. It is what you know the Bible actually says that will help you in your life. You must know it for yourself. So *now* you know the first commission for any believer.

In verse 17 of chapter 16 of the Book of Mark, Jesus said, "And these signs shall follow them that believe; In my name shall they cast out devils." Do you do it?

After studying very carefully the Book of Mark, sixteenth chapter, following an order that God gave me to go study that chapter, I found out it was my duty as a believer to cast out devils. But I didn't think that the Lord would give me a duty to cast the Devil out right away. I thought He would give me a lot more training, but He says, "Just believe what you read, because the great commission is the greatest words that were ever spoken out of My mouth. Because the Gospel brings life to a human being, casting out devils in My name is My first commission for the believer."

Casting out devils brings a healing to the inner man. Jesus has taught me since then that every human being is going to be full of something, and if one is full of the Devil, get the devils out and get him filled up with God. You may not even know what's wrong with you, but if you do stupid and crazy things you are full of the Devil. You need to come to Jesus and be set free by God's power. And you can be free. Oh, it's so good to be free.

3

The College Girl
Thrown Out of School

After Jesus told me to go study the sixteenth chapter of the Book of Mark and after He showed me my duty as a believer, the next Sunday I went to church. On Sunday morning when the service was over I started out the side door, and the pastor said to me, "Brother Hayes, can I talk to you for a minute?"

I turned around, and he said, "You have visited so many colleges and universities in this country, and have much experience in working with young people. I have a college girl I would like for you to counsel with. Would you be willing to talk to her?"

I said, "Sure, I'll talk with her and help her if I can. When would you like for me to talk with her?"

He said, "Well, right now, if you have time. She is sitting back here in the church." And I looked back there and the last few people were walking out of the doors of the sanctuary, and this girl was sitting alone.

I walked back and sat on the same bench that she was on. She was sitting there with her head down. She didn't look up. She didn't look around. She just sat there. So I casually just began to make conversation with her, and she would not answer back. So I just made further conversation.

I guess I had been talking about two minutes, and there was nobody in the church except her and me, when all of a sudden, while I was talking, she just got up and walked out of the sanctuary and left me sitting there. She never did say a word to me—hello, good-bye, or anything.

When she walked out, the Spirit of the Lord that was within me began to deal with me concerning her problem, and I went out to the front of the church and I saw the pastor and I said, "Pastor, I'm not trying to interfere with this girl's life, because I don't even know her, but has this girl got problems of keeping men away from her?"

He said, "The worst I have ever seen in my life. But I can't help her. I have talked with her, but I can't help her. She has been thrown out of college and is seeking help, but she has found none."

I said, "Well, the Lord began to deal with me concerning her problem, so I will be praying about the matter and see what happens."

This was on Sunday morning. Wednesday night meeting I went back again to the prayer meeting service—and I was sitting there and the preacher preached, and he asked everybody to bow his head, and he prayed. And when he got through praying, I raised my head up, and there this same girl was—bowed down on her knees at the altar of the church—and I got up out of my seat and went down and knelt beside her and just began to pray for her.

In a few minutes, some people began to come and gather around and pray, and I guess I prayed for about fifteen minutes. Then I just didn't feel like praying anymore, so I got up off my knees and went back to my seat. I guess there were ten or fifteen people around her praying, and they had been praying some forty-five minutes, I guess. I was just sitting there in my own seat minding my own business, when all of a sudden the Holy Ghost that lives in me began to manifest Himself, and the power of God began to rise up out of me.

He began to remind me how He had spoken to me a week before in my car. I could begin to see myself driving that car the moment He spoke to me and told me to go study the last chapter of the Book of Mark, and I began to relive my driving to get the Bible, and opening the Bible to the last chapter of the Book of Mark,—and, as I started studying the first verse, my coming down to the part where Jesus appeared to Mary Magdalene first when He came out of the tomb.

I recalled how a great wave of the love of God flowed over me, and how I came on down to the great commission in the fifteenth chapter and He said to me, "These are the most important words that ever came out of My mouth." And how I came down to verse 17, where Jesus said, "These signs shall follow them that believe; In my name shall they cast out devils. . . . "

By this time hot tears were flowing from my eyes. My face was a mass of flooded tears, gushing up from the inside as the Holy Ghost that was in me began to manifest Himself.

Then He began to remind me of the woman in California quivering on the floor, whom Mr. Murphy had come to rescue, how he had said, "In Jesus name, come out of her," how I agreed with him in the command, how the glorious presence of Jesus came and set the woman free, and how she had looked like an angel. And I sat there in a mass of tears flooding from me, and all I could see before me was the sixteenth chapter of the Book of Mark, the seventeenth verse rolling around in front of my eyes.

Where Jesus said, "These signs shall follow them that

23

believe: In my name shall they cast out devils," I said, "Jesus, I was raised in the First Baptist Church, and they didn't teach me to cast out devils"—and He immediately said to me, "The sixteenth chapter of the Book of Mark DOES."

You see, it doesn't make any difference what they teach where you go to church—it is what the Bible teaches; that is the only thing that God has anything to do with. God has not failed us as human beings, as His children, but we have mightily failed God by trying to go our own way and not obeying His Word. If you can read, you can read for yourself to see what that chapter teaches, what Jesus says in verse 17 chapter 16 of the Book of Mark.

I said, "Jesus, I do love You, Lord." I said, "Jesus, I do love You."

And He said very plainly, "Yes, you have been going around the country, standing before banquets, standing before conventions, standing before churches, standing before crusades, telling people that you love Me. Tonight, I demand that you show Me."

You see, my friend, it is one thing to *tell* Jesus that you love Him, but it is another thing to *show* Him that you love Him. If you say you love Him with your mouth but you refuse to obey a command from Him, then you have a sick love. You have a love that God is not pleased with. God wants His Word to be obeyed. He is not interested in your telling Him that you love Him with your mouth but refuse to carry out a duty and obey His Word.

God said don't be just hearers of the Word, but be doers thereof. Any man, Jesus said, that is ashamed of the Gospel—any man, Jesus said, that is ashamed of Me and of My Word—when he stands before Me on Judgment Day,

I will be ashamed of him. Verse 17 chapter 16 of the Book of Mark is Jesus' Word. So I am warning you, you had better not be ashamed of it.

But I have to admit to you the truth: I was ashamed of it. I didn't want to do it, but Jesus said to me, "You have been going around the country telling the people that you love Me. Tonight, I demand that you show Me by obeying My command in the sixteenth chapter and the seventeenth verse of the Book of Mark."

Then I said to Him, "Jesus, is that California deal the only training I get?"

He plainly and quickly let me know, "That's all you need. All you have to do is obey the seventeenth verse of the sixteenth chapter of the Book of Mark; and when you obey that verse, all you do is say in My name 'come out,' and it will come out."

But I said, "Lord, there are a lot of good Christians praying for that girl. They probably could talk You into helping her."

Immediately, again, He said to me, still flooding me supernaturally with floods of tears, "Oh, no they can't; they are not going to talk Me into helping her—that is not My command. I didn't say in My name *pray* devils out. Devils have taken this girl over. I said, in My name, *cast* them out. I didn't say *pray*. I said *cast*."

I said, "Jesus, I have got a lot of friends in this place, please don't make me do this here. . . . "

And immediately the Devil said to me, "You had better not go up there and obey the seventeenth verse of the sixteenth chapter of the Book of Mark. You had better not obey that in front of your friends. What if you get up there and that thing doesn't go out? Then you'll get into an embarrassing mess just like California. Remember how you were embarrassed in front of that congregation in California? When you didn't know what to do?"

The Devil kept trying to talk to me and tell me " . . . and you don't know what to do *now*. You never have done this before. It won't work. You had better not get up there and go do that. It won't work."

Jesus kept reminding me, "You have been going around the country telling people that you love Me; tonight I demand that you show Me."

After His melting a lot of my natural strength, and after His mighty healing power and His mighty delivering power flowed through my mind and through my head, and through my spirit and through my body, burning the shaft out of me, I said to Him, "Jesus, I'll do it. Because I do love You, Jesus, and I'll do it."

I said, "Jesus, if You will condition me through the power of the Holy Spirit to do this job, I will get up out of my seat and go up there and do it, even if they throw me out of this place."

Immediately, the Holy Spirit in me began to let me get mad. You might say, "Mad at what?" Mad at the Devil. I looked back up there at the altar of God and I saw that girl, seeking, seeking, seeking for help, but finding none. And I began to say, "You dirty devil that has wrecked that beautiful girl's life, that has got that nineteen-year-old college girl thrown out of school, caused her mother and father embarrassment—for what you have put that girl through, I hate you. I hate you, and you are not going to destroy this girl. I am not going to let you. I hate you— you dirty lying devil."

Jesus said to me, "I love that girl, and don't you ever

forget it. And I love all of the ones like her. And I want you to love her. And I want you to hate the devil that has wrecked her life. You are not fighting that girl, you are fighting the devil that has tried to wreck her life and has tried to separate her from Me. You are fighting him, not her. I love that girl and all of the ones like her."

I sat there a few minutes longer and I got so mad I couldn't stand it any longer. I came up out of my seat, bold, just like the king of the jungle, like a lion roaring through the jungle. I walked up there and got in front of that girl, and about the time I walked up in front of her some man said maybe we should have her stand up.

I spoke out with a loud voice like a man from another world, and I said, "That's right. Have her stand up right now, because God is going to set her free."

They had her stand up, and I reached out and put one hand on one side of her head and put the other hand lightly on the other side of her head, and I said, "You foul spirit that has wrecked this girl's life, in the name of the Lord Jesus Christ, I command you to come out of her."

And the moment I said that, her body went back through the air and she hit the floor flat on her back, and she began to speak in the most beautiful language that I ever heard, and her hands went immediately straight up in the air, and over her face came the glow of an angel, and the tears were streaming down her face—and the power of God fell in that place and people all over the floor began to dance, to dance, and to dance, and to dance.

And her father, who was an accountant, a CPA, stood in the middle of the floor, broke and began to cry and weep and weep—and, oh, how Jesus changed that girl's life that night. And after a while, rejoicing in God, she got up and began to love everybody, began to hug everybody. That old wretched look across her face had changed completely. Through one statement, through one verse of Scripture, because I had obeyed the seventeenth verse of the sixteenth chapter of the Book of Mark. I had merely said, "In Jesus' name, you foul spirit, come out of her," and it left in a split second. It was gone and she was completely healed.

Several weeks later they asked me to come to her wedding. She met a young man and they fell in love with each other, and I went and read the Bible at her wedding. The same pastor preached her wedding and married the couple, but they wanted me to read the Bible in the wedding ceremony or at the beginning of the ceremony, and it was beautiful. Oh, the power of God that set her free! "In Jesus' name, shall they cast out devils." That is to every believer, Jesus said, in the sixteenth chapter, the seventeenth verse of the Book of Mark. I want to ask you a question: Are you a believer? I want to ask you another question: Are you casting out devils? If not, why not? I would suggest to you that you study the sixteenth chapter of the Book of Mark—and especially your duty in the seventeenth verse.

It is one thing to read about devils; it is another thing to cast them out. Do you do it? As a believer, you *can* do it—and great freedom in God will come to you if you will make a devil leave in Jesus' name. You don't ask a devil anything, you tell him: *Get out.*

4

The Boy Who Set Schoolhouses on Fire

One day I was sitting in my office working when I received a telephone call from a friend of mine. He said to me, "I have a most unusual case. I have a thirteen-year-old boy with me who cannot go to school. They won't allow him to go to school anyplace, because he tries to set the schoolhouses on fire. And I am calling you to ask if you think you could help him."

I said, "No, I don't think I can help him; I know I can."

You see, you either know or you don't know. We are not playing guessing games. Jesus is real and the Devil is real, and you have to know that God's power is stronger than the Devil's power—and you have to know that in Jesus' name the Devil has to obey you. He doesn't have any choice. The only choice the Devil has is what you give him. And I just don't give any, because I know that God's power is stronger than the Devil's power.

My friend said, "We can't find anybody to help him; that is the reason I'm calling you."

They were about ninety-five miles away. They wanted to bring him to my office to be ministered to. I said to them, "Well, leave now and come to my office and we will have lunch together."

I knew that I could do a better job with this young man if he became a friend of mine and I could teach him how to fight the Devil. It is one thing to be free of the Devil's power, and it is another thing to stay free. And you stay free by resisting the Devil. The Devil can never destroy you if you resist him.

You see, I knew that I was going to bind up, "in Jesus' name," the power that made him set the schoolhouses on fire. In the meantime, I just asked the Lord to give me wisdom to know how to pray for this young man, and I asked the Lord to let us be friends. I wasn't interested in being a friend of the spirit that made him set the school-houses on fire; I wanted to be a friend of the young man so I could get that spirit out of him. I wanted the young man to trust me, because I know the Devil doesn't trust me and I know he doesn't like me. There is no love lost, because I don't like him either. That is the reason I use the name of Jesus and cast him out. I have no intention of letting some devil take over a thirteen-year-old boy and wreck his life so he can't even go to school.

So, in a few hours, they came to my office. We went to the Holiday Inn and all had lunch, and the Lord allowed him and me to sit together. I didn't mention anything. I spent at least an hour and a half making friends with him and just carrying on a conversation. He was a very smart, intelligent, nice-looking young lad, very well-mannered. You could tell his parents had taught him well.

After we finished our lunch, I said, "Well, let us take a little ride. We will ride over and I will show you the church."

So we went to the church. We looked around the sanctuary for a few minutes, and I told my friend to make arrangements with the ladies to go off by themselves, and he and the young lad and I would go into the church office. So we sat in the church office and began to talk, and I had been praying for wisdom.

As the conversation went on, we began to talk about doing things that we didn't want to do. I began to talk and the Lord began to give me the words to say about when I was a teenager and would do things against my parents, doing things behind my parents' back, and how I didn't like myself and I knew it was wrong. And I looked over to the young lad and I said, "Did you ever do anything like that—that you knew was wrong after you did it?"

Very humbly he said, "Yes, I've done things that I knew weren't right, but some things in my life I just have to do."

At that moment he began to look strange, staring down at the floor, and he said, "Sometimes I have to do things; I don't want to do them, but there is something that makes me do them, and I have to. I just have to do them. It seems that I have no choice. I just have to do them."

Then he looked up and said, "I know what you are talking about, because after I do a thing like that I am always sorry and wonder why I did it."

You see, when you are dealing with the Devil, you have to be smarter than the Devil. The Holy Spirit that lives within you is smarter and stronger than the Devil himself; but in some cases, you must pray for wisdom. The Bible says let him that lacketh wisdom ask for it; and when you ask Jesus for something, it will be granted unto you.

At this moment in our conversation I just merely said, "I was glad to get rid of those powers in my life that would try to drive me to do things that I knew weren't right, and you feel so good inside when you are not controlled by that power that drives you to do wrong. I imagine, young fellow, that you would like for that power never to visit your life again, wouldn't you?"

He said, "Yes, I would."

I said, "Well, let's just all have prayer. It is always good to pray—because, young fellow, you do realize that Jesus loves you, don't you?"

He was a very nice polite young fellow and he said, "Yes, I realize that Jesus loves me."

"So let's all go to prayer, " I said, "and ask Jesus, the One that loves us, to help us."

He agreed, so we began to pray a simple prayer. And as I took him by the hands and began to pray, I began just to take authority over that power of darkness that would try to drive this young fellow into doing wrong, and I began to talk to this power and I began to command it to stop working in his life, in Jesus' name.

I just got the young fellow to say, "Jesus, I'm sorry for the sins that I have committed and the wrong that I have done," and asked Jesus to forgive him for it.

The Bible tells in chapter 16 of the Book of Matthew, verse 18, that Jesus said, "And I say also unto thee, That thou art Peter, and upon this rock I will build my church; and the gates of hell shall not prevail against it." Realizing that I was a part of this church and, now that this young man had repented of his sins, he too was a part of the church, the Devil had no more power over him.

It is just that simple—but you have to bind that power up, because Jesus said in chapter 16 verse 19 of the Book of Matthew, "And I will give unto thee the keys of the kingdom of heaven: and whatsoever thou shalt bind on earth shall be bound in heaven: and whatsoever thou shall loose on earth shall be loosed in heaven." I knew that I had the keys to unlock the right lock of power, to bind that power of darkness up where it couldn't wreck this young man's life.

So in Jesus' name, I bound up the Devil's power that was trying to destroy him, and following the instructions that Jesus had given unto the church and unto me in chapter 16 verse 19 of the Book of Matthew, I bound the power up in Jesus' name and commanded him not to operate against this young fellow anymore. I commanded him to stop, and I commanded him to come out of him and let this young man's life go free.

When the prayer was over, the young man thanked me and said that he appreciated the prayer, and I told him we were not going to let the Devil, or that forceful power that drives you to do things, we were not going to let it operate through him anymore—and I began to teach him from the Book of James how to resist that power so that the Devil will flee from you.

I said, "Young man, the very next time that power comes to you and tries to drive you to do something that is wrong, I want you to say, according to James, chapter 4 verse 7, I want you to say, 'Jesus, I love you'—and that verse says, 'Submit yourselves therefore to God. Resist the devil, and he will flee from you.' I want you to obey that and resist, and begin to tell that power that you belong to God, and that you love Jesus and resist that power. Will you do it?"

He said, "I will."

We walked around the sanctuary and talked for a while —and I guess maybe thirty minutes later, when they began to leave, I wanted to pray the blessings of God upon his life. So I prayed the blessings of God upon him, and sent him out on his way home.

Sometime later I went to Atlanta, Georgia, to hold a week's teaching seminar for Reverend Horton in the Church of God. This young man came to the service and brought his father and mother. He was really going on with God. They came and thanked me and told me what a change had come to his life. They began to come to the services, and one night this young fellow came forth and received the baptism of the Holy Spirit and power. The last letter I received from him was just a few weeks ago, saying that Jesus had called him to preach the Gospel.

I am so thankful that God's power is available for anybody, and that anybody can be free of anything in Jesus' name if he will learn how to resist the Devil and fight him. But you *must* fight the Devil, and you must do it in Jesus' name, because when you repent of your sins and ask Jesus to come into your heart, you become a part of the church —and the church of the Lord Jesus Christ is the place where Jesus dedicated all of His power, and it is up to us what we do with it.

We have all power on earth that we need to make all powers of darkness flee from our lives. When temptation begins to come to you, immediately start resisting in Jesus' name, and begin to yield yourselves and submit yourselves therefore to God. And tell Jesus that you love Him, and begin to worship Him. Begin to say, "Jesus, Jesus, Jesus," and you will find deliverance for your life.

5

The Girl Who Danced in the Woods at Night

One weekend I received a telephone call at my home from a lay leader who was a member of the Full Gospel Businessmen's Chapter in Chattanooga, Tennessee, and he said to me, "I was answering the telephone last night for our toll-free line in Chattanooga and I received a call from a young lady who can't find anyone to help her, and my heart went out to her. She tries to kill her relatives. I have called her relatives and talked to them about her and they have informed me that she tried to kill her aunt yesterday with a knife when her aunt's back was turned, and I felt like calling you to ask you if you could help this girl."

Of course, I said, "No, I don't think I can help her; I *know* I can."

Once Jesus teaches you how to take authority over the Devil that hates the human race, and once Jesus teaches you how to cast out devils, then you don't have to go on asking people what they think about it—because, you see, it doesn't make any difference what people think about anything. It is what God's Word actually says that ever matters. Nothing else matters. And Jesus said, "In My name cast out devils, if you are a believer."

So the man said to me, "We would like to bring her for you to minister to. What time can we make an appointment?"

I said, "Well, meet me at the church at 6:00 o clock on Sunday afternoon."

So we met at the church at 6:00 p.m. They came in—one woman and two men and a very beautiful young lady, sixteen years of age, wearing a miniskirt, with long straight beautiful hair.

She was a very beautiful girl. At a distance she looked like Miss Teenage America herself. As I approached them they introduced the young lady to me and I said, "It is nice to know you."

She looked at me and said, "I will kill you."

I said, "No, you can't kill me."

And she said, "But I try to kill people."

And I said, "Well, you won't kill me, because I don't die so easy"—I immediately came back at her with a strong statement to find out what kind of strength this demon had who had her possessed. I said to her, "Do you want me to pray for you?"

Quickly she answered with a strong voice, "No, I don't want you to pray for me. What's wrong with you ? I don't want you to pray for me. No, I don't want you to pray for me."

So I calmed down and just began to casually talk about things. We walked together on the other side of the church where the Sunday school rooms are, and we went into one of the Sunday school rooms. We were all standing in there talking, and the young lady was standing up. I asked, "Are you going to let me pray for you?"

She said, "No, I'm not going to let you pray for me. What's wrong with you, wanting to pray for me? There is nothing wrong with me, and you are not going to pray for me."

So I saw that if I ever got to pray for her, I would have to pray whether she wanted me to or not. So I just quietly, slowly worked my way in front of her—and I didn't act like I was going to pray for her, just talk with her a little bit.

Immediately I reached up quickly and grabbed her by the head, and I said with a loud voice, "In Jesus' name, come out of her. In Jesus' name, I say, come out of her. Turn this girl loose and come out of her."

Immediately her body just lost its strength. She began to melt to the floor. She got about halfway to the floor and suddenly she jumped. Her body rose up into the air, and her hands and arms went out, and great strength came into her. She looked at me so hard and said, "Leave me alone. I don't want you to pray. Don't pray. What do you mean, trying to pray for me? I don't want you to pray for me. What's wrong with you? Don't pray."

I saw immediately that the demon that had her possessed was not going to leave easily, so I turned around and told the two men to step outside.

We left her alone with the lady, stepped outside into the hallway and into the prayer room, and I said, "Now, men, it may be easy to get her free, and it may not be, but I know that that thing will try to fight me, and once I start into this, I'm not going to give up. Are you men willing to stay here, even two, three, or four hours, if it takes it? Because those things will have to come out of her, and we'll have to pray God's blessing upon her and get her filled with God, and they are not going to turn loose of her easy. They have been there for a long time and they think they own her body. They think it is their house forever."

The men said to me, "We are willing to stay as long as it takes for the girl to get help."

"Well, she'll get help," I said, "because Jesus loves her, and His mighty power will help her if we follow His instructions—and His instructions are, if you are a believer, for you to cast out devils (Mark 16:17). That is the first commission for any believer; and any believer of the Lord Jesus Christ can cast out devils if he just knows that.

"But you can't be afraid and cast them out. You can't be a doubter and cast them out, because you see the devils know you. They know how much you believe in God's power, and they know if you will obey the Scriptures or not. If you don't obey the Scriptures, they don't obey you. Let's go back into the room."

We went back into the room, and the lady we left with her said to us, on the side, "When you all left the room a few minutes ago, the young lady said to me, 'When he grabbed me by the head and commanded these things to come out, there was something black—he was big and tall, I saw him. He was a lot taller than I am, and I know that he came out of my body and stood in front of me looking at me, and I felt myself sinking—and immediately he stretched his hands out and jumped back on me, and power came into me. He was so big and black standing before me."

I said to her, "Sure, that is why I commanded it to come out in Jesus' name. It came out; and when I stopped, her body was already sinking onto the floor, and he jumped back into her."

About this time the Sunday night service started in the church, and they began to sing. We decided to go in and enjoy the church service and take the young lady in and further minister to her after church. So we went in and sat down on the front bench of the church. I was sitting next to the young lady. The pastor was behind the pulpit getting ready to introduce his guest speaker, who was a young evangelist from Florida. The pastor was making some remarks about Jesus.

The young lady whispered to me and told me, "Tell that man up there talking to be quiet. I don't want to hear him."

"No, you be quiet," I said. "He is the pastor and the head of this church and he doesn't have to be quiet. You be quiet."

And she said, "I don't want to hear what he is saying."

I said, "It doesn't make any difference what you want; you can't tell the pastor of the church to be quiet."

About this time the pastor introduced the young visiting evangelist, his guest speaker for the night, and he got up and began to open the Bible and began to read the Bible. And that really shook her up. She immediately said to me, "Tell him I said to be quiet."

She put both hands over her ears, squeezing the side of her head, while he was reading the Bible. She told me later on that when she did that, his reading got louder. She could just hear it roaring, blasting at her. From the natural standpoint, you would say a person couldn't hear who had his ears stopped up, but she said his reading of the Bible really got loud when she stopped her ears up.

After a while she took her hands off her ears and leaned over to me and said with an audible voice, and some people could hear her, "Tell him I said to stop reading that. What he is saying is not true, and I don't want to hear it."

I said, "Be quiet, young lady; he is reading the Bible."

She said, "It is not true. Tell him I said to stop."

I just sat there and told her to be quiet.

She sat there a few seconds and said to me again, "If you don't tell him to stop reading that, I am going to scream, I am going to scream, I can't stand it. I'm going to scream, because what he is saying is not true. It is a lie. It is not true. There is no point to his standing up there reading that, because it is not true." And her voice turned, actually sounding pitiful, and she said, "Please tell him to stop saying that, because that is not true what he is saying."

I said, "No, young lady, I'm not going to tell him to stop. Now be quiet."

In a few seconds she said, "I'm thirsty. I've got to get some water. Please, I've got to have some water."

I have noticed many times, devils are always wanting me to give them a drink. I guess they know where they are going to spend eternity, and they want to get all the water they can while they are here doing their damage, because the time is coming when there will be no water. They will all have to go back and be cast into the lake which burneth with fire and brimstone—but they are not in that lake of fire now; they are roaming back and forth through the air of this world, seeking whom they may devour, because they are here for only three reasons: to kill, to steal, and to destroy. And this includes you or anybody else that they can talk into listening to them.

She was causing such a disturbance in the church that I agreed to get her a drink of water. I said, "There is a water fountain downstairs. I will go with you."

So we went out the door by the front of the church and went downstairs. As we started down the stairs, she immediately turned to me and said, "Please, I want you to go back in and sit down and enjoy it. I don't want you to go with me. I want to go get a drink of water alone."

I said, "No, I am going with you to get some water."

She said, "Don't you understand? I don't want you to go; I want to go alone."

And I said with authority to her, "It doesn't make any difference what you want, I am going anyway." And she said okay.

We went on to the water fountain. She got a drink first. When she finished, I bent over to get a drink, and I heard footsteps running. I turned around and she was running across the basement of the church, heading for the outside door.

I took off after her. She was running like a wild turkey. I finally caught her right before she reached the outside entrance, and I saw that she was going to get out the door or beat me to the entrance, so I just took a flying leap through the air and tackled her. Just like a University of Tennessee football player would do when Tennessee was playing Georgia Tech.

Somebody had given her a Bible, and her Bible went one way and her pocketbook went another way. We both landed flat on the floor, and she got up fighting. She tried to tear me all to pieces. She tried to kick me, she tried to hit me in the face. I mean she was turning at me with great strength. You wouldn't think a cute little doll like this girl would think about fighting, but she fought like a champion wrestler, or like a wildcat that had just been turned out of a cage.

I finally got her arms and I held them—and it was all I could do to hold them. I started to pull her over to the

Sunday school room where we were previously. I got her to the door, but I couldn't get her in; she was too strong. And she said to me, "Turn my arms loose and I will open the door for you. Just trust me. I'll open the door for you."

Well, anybody ought to have sense enough to know that you can't trust the Devil. But you know, the Devil always hangs himself—so I turned one arm loose.

She acted like she was going to open up the door. Then she went and tried to slug me. So I grabbed her arm back and tried to twist her around and hold her against the wall, and tried to get both of her arms real quick in one of my hands.

I got her in the room and closed the door. As soon as I closed the door, the fight was over. She stopped, just as calm as could be. She walked over to a picture that was on the wall and stood there just as calmly, with her back to me, looking at the picture. And she said, "I bet you think the Devil is in me, don't you?"

And I said to her, "Well, what do you think?"

And she said with a trembling voice, "If he is, I wish that he would leave me alone."

"Good," I said, "I am glad you want him to leave you alone."

And then I knew that, deep down inside her, she was searching for relief from this powerful force that had her possessed.

Then we sat down, and I began to talk with her about her past life. She told me that when she was a small child her mother had been a prostitute, and she said that was the very reason why she would never marry.

"I have never given my body to any man," she said. "I have been on dope for over three years, and I have traveled lots of miles, but no man has ever touched my body, because I fight them—and I am strong. I hate men because I saw as a child how different men treated my mother. My mother was a prostitute. She was beautiful." She showed me a picture of her mother. She was a very beautiful woman.

She said, "My father belonged to the Hell's Angels, and he used to lock my sister and me in a closet and close the door and stand outside laughing, because we hated darkness and we were afraid. And we would stand in the closet screaming for him to let us out, but he would stand outside and laugh until we screamed so hard and so long that we both passed out in the closet."

I thought to myself, "Dear Lord in Heaven, no wonder this girl is in such bad shape, the treatment she has received in the past."

She said, "No man will ever touch me. Many men have tried, but I fight them. I have had them chase me into the lake, and I would fight them out on the lake—and I never am going to let any man touch me.

"One day," she went on, "my mother cut her throat, and the blood was streaming down her; and she fell on the floor and reached up with her bloody hands and said, 'Come on, go with me. Let me cut your throat. Come and go with me.' But they finally got to her and saved her."

Of course, after counseling with the people that brought her and meeting her relatives, I knew this girl had really been through a terrible childhood.

After a while the service was over, and the people that brought her came back in, and we were all sitting there talking. And we talked for a few minutes, so I didn't even let her know that I was going to pray for her. I walked back around pretty close in front of her, and quickly I grabbed her head again, and I pulled her face pretty close to mine, and I began to say with a loud voice and with authority, "In the name of the Lord Jesus Christ, I command you to come out of her. I command you to let this girl's body go free. I command you to let this girl's mind go free. You are not going to destroy this girl. I'm not going to let you destroy her. In Jesus' name I command you to come out of her. I said, in Jesus' name let her go free, and come out of her."

I must have said that real fast, and with authority, some twenty times or more—and then I just all of a sudden turned her loose. When I did, she was quivering like a sick puppy.

She had tried to fight me for the first few seconds to get loose, when I had begun to pray with her, but I held on tightly and wouldn't let her go—and I kept on commanding it to come out of her, and I could sense the break of that power that had her. When I turned her loose, she immediately went to the corner of the building whimpering, making a funny noise just like a pup. She looked like she was half scared to death, quivering, with her hands up towards her chin.

About this time the young evangelist from Florida who spoke in the church that night walked in with his Bible (it is just wonderful to know that the Holy Ghost is in you to guide you and to teach you the truth; He knows more in five seconds that we know in five years) and immediately the Word of the Lord came unto me, saying, "She hates the Bible. Have him read the Bible."

So I told the young man to open up his Bible and start reading loud and with authority. He was fumbling around and didn't know what to read, and I said, "Read anything out of the New Testament. Just open it up and begin to read, like you were standing there reading it to a class. Read it with authority. Read it with a strong voice."

He opened up and began to read strong and loud, and I said, "Read it louder and read it stronger." And he kept on reading it.

After about five minutes, he began to stop reading, and I said, "Don't stop. Keep on reading, read more—because, you see, the patience of God wears the Devil out."

He began to read more and more. She was still in the corner of the room quivering, and I began to look over towards her, and I saw a teardrop running down one cheek. In a few seconds I saw another teardrop on the other cheek. More teardrops began to flood her face, and she began to melt slowly to the floor, inch by inch; and he was still reading the Bible, loud and with authority.

Some three or four minutes went by and she was down as far as a kneeling position. In another couple of minutes, inch by inch, her face was on the floor, and by this time she was sobbing and crying openly. And on the floor she must have cried fifteen minutes.

I have taught the Bible on university campuses, I have taught the Bible on college campuses, in university class rooms, in most all kinds of churches, at banquets—and I have seen a lot of conversions—but I believe that this was the most beautiful conversion that I had ever seen in my life.

After sobbing on the floor some fifteen minutes, she raised her head up slowly and looked at me, and her face looked like she had dipped it in a pail of water. Her face looked like an angel's, and for the first time a real sweet smile, full of compassion, came across her face, and the glory of God was all over her, surging through her body.

Her mind had been washed clean. As she looked at me for a few seconds and reached her little hands up trembling under the power of God, she got up slowly off the floor and came straight over to me, and she looked just like an angel. She reached up and put her arms around my neck and stood there holding on to me for some ten minutes, with the Spirit of God surging through her body, laughing, crying, crying, laughing, crying, rejoicing in Jesus, shedding tears of joy and thanking Jesus.

Now she is happy and now I am happy. All of the devils are gone. I have been washed clean, as by a stream of water bubbling up in my innermost being, flowing through my whole body. Then, in a few minutes, we all thanked the Lord together for what He had done for this girl, and I said, "Well, let's all go to one of my restaurants and have some pizza. Do you like pizza, young lady?"

She said, "Yes, I do." And she told the people that had brought her, "I want to ride to the restaurant with Mr. Hayes. I love him so much, I want to ride with him. Please let me ride to the restaurant with him."

I said, "Okay, young lady. You can ride with me, and they can follow us with their car." So she got in my car and we began to go towards one of my restaurants for a midnight pizza. It was about midnight by this time.

On the way to the restaurant she began to talk to me and said, "Please help me, I wouldn't take anything in the world for what I have in me right now. Please help me. Don't let those people take me back to my room in Chattanooga. I have pictures of demons and the Devil in my room, all over the walls. That is where my dope is at. That

46

is where the demons come and get me at night. They make me go into the woods and dance. Thank God I can sleep in the bed tonight. I haven't slept in a bed in over four months at night. They make me go into the woods and dance for hours each night. I sleep during the day, but I roam by night. Please don't let them take me back to my room."

I said, "Well, we'll see, young lady. We will talk it over when we get to the restaurant."

She said, "I need somebody to help me. I just love you people so much. Oh, what a thrilling life it would be if a person could live with people like you who have love in them. Oh, what I feel in my body now. I don't want to lose this love."

I said, "Young lady, you don't have to lose that love. That is the love of Jesus. Jesus said, 'I will never leave you, I will never forsake you, and I will be with you, and I will be in you, even to the end of the world.' (*See* Matthew 28:20.) Jesus will never leave you, but I want to teach you tonight how to live so you can keep Him in you, because He loves you with a love that never fails, and it is your right to enjoy that love all the days of your life. We will talk about it at the restaurant."

We all got to the restaurant, and she could hardly talk for rejoicing—still crying and still thrilled for what Jesus had done for her. When they brought the pizza, she said, "I just don't want to eat very much, because I am so full of the love of Jesus. I am so thankful for what Jesus has done for me. I didn't think a person could feel like this. I didn't know a person could love everybody. I don't want to kill anybody. I don't want to harm anybody. I just want to love everybody."

Then I told her in front of the other people, "I don't want you to be afraid to go back to your room." I told them she had said she was afraid to go back to her room because she had pictures of demons around her walls and things of the Devil, and that room is where they come and visit her and drive her into the woods at night to dance.

"I want you to promise me something," I told the others, "or I can go do it myself. When you take her back to her room tonight, I want you to walk in there and tear all of those pictures off the wall and tear them up. Then take them out and destroy them, and take every idol, take every occult sign, every Ouija board, every picture of the Devil or of demons out of that room, and throw them away. And I want you all to stand in the middle of the room and hold hands, and lay hands on this girl in that room and pray, and bind those foul spirits up where they can't operate in that room. Bind them up in Jesus' name. Tell the Devil that she is free from his power, and plead the blood of Jesus over that room. She belongs to Jesus now. She was saved tonight from the power of darkness through the blood of Jesus."

And I said to the girl, "Don't be afraid, young lady. The Devil and all of his demons and workers are not going to drive you into the woods tonight to dance, because these people are going to bind that spirit up and pray in your room."

And the girl said, "Well, all right, if you say so."

I said, "Well, the reason I say so is that Jesus said so. He said so in the Bible, that whatever you bind on earth shall be bound in heaven, whatever you leave loose in earth shall be loosed in heaven. We are not going to leave anything loose that belongs to the Devil in your room. We

48

are going to throw it away and do away with it." So they left and took her home.

The next night I was speaking in a place in Chattanooga, and she got them to bring her to the service. The moment I walked in she came running with a smile on her face, just like a little bouncy ideal American teenager. She threw her arms around me and said, "Jesus has been so good to me last night and today. Thank you for praying for me. It is wonderful to be free. It is so wonderful to be normal. I've got something to tell you. Can we go out on the balcony so I can tell you?"

This place where I was speaking had a balcony, so before the service we walked out there for a few minutes; and she began to thank me for taking the time to minister to her, and to tell me how beautiful that day had been in her life. That it was the most thrilling day that she had ever lived. That her life was full of joy and full of peace, and that she wasn't afraid. And she made a statement that I will never forget:

She said, "Thank you for wrestling with me. I found in the Bible where Jacob wrestled with an angel. That puts me in mind of you and me wrestling on the floor—Jesus' power wrestling with the Devil's power."

I said, "Yes, the power of God that lives in me was fighting the power of the Devil that lived in you, fighting him for your soul and your very life—because, you see, young lady, Jesus loves you."

And she said, "I know, I know; and it is so wonderful. I don't want to loose this love that I have found."

"No," I said, "this is the most valuable thing that you will ever come in contact with in this life. So stay with

Him and resist the Devil, and resist and fight the power of darkness.''

It was time for the service. We went back in and I spoke that night, and I will never forget that she began to rejoice in the Lord, and how the power of the Holy Spirit was surging through her again and blessing her.

I would like to stop here and tell you that it is good to see people set free from the Devil's power, but what they have to be taught is how to stay free, because the Devil is not dead, and he doesn't give up easily. He will return again. Say how full of God you are and he will try to tempt you, but when you tell him to flee in Jesus' name and resist him, then he goes away.

But the loneliness in people's lives can cause them to listen to the Devil when they are new Christians. I would like for you to notice what Jesus says in chapter 12 of the Book of Matthew, verses 43 and 44 and 45. Listen: Starting with verse 43 Jesus says, "When the unclean spirit is gone out of a man, he walketh through dry places, seeking rest, and findeth none." That means that the *unclean spirit* walketh through dry places, seeking rest, and findeth none. You see, foul spirits and demons are restless when they are out of the human body. They roam backwards and forwards through the air, trying to find somebody they can get in.

Verses 44 and 45 say, "Then he saith, I will return into my house from whence I came out; and when he is come, he findeth it empty, swept, and garnished. Then goeth he, and taketh with himself seven other spirits more wicked than himself, and they enter in and dwell there: and the last state of that man is worse than the first. Even so shall it be also unto this wicked generation."

As long as this young lady was with the fine people that brought her to me, she was all right. That weekend they had to leave town to go on a mission, and I left and went out on speaking engagements. When I came back into town, I received another phone call from the same man, the lay leader from Chattanooga, and he said to me, "The young lady was all right until Saturday. The Devil told her on Saturday that we were all gone now, and that nobody loved her except him. He told her that we didn't love her —if we had we would never have left. And the Devil told her, 'You know what sensation there is in the needle—and you know the feelings you would have when you shoot the needle. Go quickly and get the needle, and put it in your arm. They don't love you. If they did, they would never have left you. They are gone. They don't love you. I love you. Go get the needle and shoot it quickly. Don't wait. Do it now.' And his power visited her so strongly that she went and got the needle and shot it on Saturday."

We were starting a youth crusade with a young evangelist who had just preached around the world. He was from San Diego, California. I had worked some with this young man, and I knew that he also had a good ministry. He also believed in taking authority over the Devil, so I told the man to bring her to the service, and he invited her.

She remembered the feeling that the Lord gave her when He saved her. Now she had lost it, but she wanted to be restored to Jesus. The Devil knew that she was coming, and he told her to bring me two things.

He said, "I want you to take Norvel Hayes all of your dope except the needle—don't take him the needle. Take him all of your marijuana, take him all of your pills, but don't take him your needle. And I want you to put a double-edged razor blade in your back pocket—and when he begins to pray for you, I want you to cut his throat."

So I was sitting in church, and the people came in. She came in and sat by me and she said to me, "I brought you two things tonight."

She handed me a little bag with stuff wrapped up in it, and I opened the bag and there was her dope. Then she put her hands up to her head like some power had blocked her memory, and she said to me, "I brought you two things, but I can't remember what the other one was."

I would like to stop here and make one statement: Thank God for His mighty power! She said, "I can't understand why I can't remember what the other thing was that I have for you, because I know I brought you two things."

I said, "Well, maybe you will think of it later."

So the service started; and after a little while in the service she got up and left, and I noticed that she never came back. As soon as the service ended I got up and walked outside and she was sitting on the side of the steps. I walked out and began to talk with her and I said, "Why didn't you come back into the service?"

She said, "Because I didn't want to."

She looked up at me so pitifully and said, "I guess you have heard what has happened to me."

I said, "Yes, I was sorry to hear it. What made you do it?"

She said, "The Devil came to me Saturday and told me that you didn't love me anymore, and the other people didn't love me anymore either. If they hadn't left me, he would have left me alone. He kept talking to me, and he kept trying to drive me to go and get the needle. He wouldn't leave me alone—and I finally just gave in. Now I feel so far away. I feel myself sinking back into the valley of darkness. But I want to ask you a favor. Please do me one favor."

I said I would if I could, and she said, "Please, tonight I want you to scream at me."

Well, that was a new one for me! "Just what do you mean, scream at you?"

She said, "That is the way I got relief before. I remember that you were screaming at me, and that you were telling something to come out of me."

I said, "Oh, I see what you mean."

"Please scream at me tonight," she said. "Please don't let me go back home without your screaming at me. Please scream at me. Will you promise me that you will scream at me some more before I go back home?"

I said, "Well, okay. I'll pray for you before you go home tonight. I know what you mean, so I will pray for you."

So several of us walked out to the back of the church, and down below there was a patch of woods. The young evangelist came out and the pastor of the church. The three of us were standing there talking—when all of a sudden she took off running into the woods.

The young evangelist went after her, but he couldn't do anything with her. She let him know in no uncertain terms that he had better get away from her. She told him that she wasn't coming back up. He talked to her for quite a long time and tried to get her to come back, and she refused. But finally she said to him, "I won't come back for anyone but Norvel. I will do whatever he tells me to do, but I'm not going to do anything for anybody else."

He came back up and told me, and I went down and

reached and got her by the hand and said, "Come on, let's go." And she came with me.

That night I had refreshments fixed at my home. The young evangelist and his wife were staying at my home, and we invited some other guests, including this young lady and the people who had brought her from Chattanooga. We went to my home for refreshments and a lot of the guests were sitting around and talking to each other. Somebody said, "Where is the young lady?" Nobody could find her.

Then somebody spotted her out in the darkness, out in the field dancing in the dark, way off from the house by herself, in the dark, dancing. So everybody came out of the house and began to watch her.

Well, it is not every day you see somebody dancing at midnight out in the field. So everyone watched her for a few minutes; and when the young evangelist went to get her, she told him, "No, I'll only come if Norvel comes after me."

So I got her. And we came back up, and were standing in the driveway talking. Somebody suggested that maybe we should go in the house and pray.

She said, "I'm not going into the house and pray. I'll only go in the house with one person, and that is Norvel —he promised to scream at me because I remembered the relief I found before when he screamed at me."

That was her term for my taking authority over the Devil in Jesus' name and commanding him to come out of her. Nevertheless, I said, "Okay, just you and I will go in the house."

"I don't want anybody else coming in," she said. "I just want to talk to him."

So I told the other people to just stay outside and fellowship for a while and we would go in the living room and talk for a few minutes.

We had been talking for a few minutes in my living room when the young evangelist walked in to see if he could help me. She wanted to know what he was doing in there.

I said, "It's okay, young lady, it's all right. He is staying here with me. It's okay." I told him just to have a seat, and we all began to talk.

In a few minutes more his wife came in, and the girl asked, "What are you doing in here?"

I said, "Well, this is the young fellow's wife. It is okay, we are all friends. We all love you. And Jesus loves you."

When I said, "Jesus loves you," she immediately got up out of her seat and ran into the hallway. We waited, but she didn't come back.

I said, "Young lady, just come on in and sit back down."

She said, "No, not if you are going to mention that name again. I'm not coming. You know what name, that name you said. I'm not coming if you talk about that name."

I said, "Well, come on back anyway."

She said, "I'm not coming."

Without hesitation, the young evangelist's wife got up. She was a daughter of a Full Gospel minister who was a pastor of a large church in Washington, and she walked in there and said, "Young lady, why don't you get back in there and talk like somebody? You put me in mind of a sideshow in a carnival, trying to get attention."

About that time, the young lady hauled back and

slapped the young minister's wife right in the face. She knocked her on the floor and jumped on her, and they began to fight and pull hair and hit each other—and I mean in the face, as hard as they could.

I told the young evangelist, "You had better go in there and get your wife. That girl will destroy her."

He said, "She won't destroy my wife. My wife will fight. She has been raised up in this and she knows what to do."

I said, "It does not make any difference what she has been raised up in. That girl is demon-possessed, and she is as strong as three girls. She is nearly as strong as I am." I kept begging and pleading with the young evangelist. "I am warning you. You had better go in there and separate them. Now, it is your wife. . . ."

By this time we could hear noises and groans. They were fighting all over the floor. So we walked in, and they really had their arms locked around each other, trying to beat each other and bite each other. We had to pull them apart. The young evangelist's wife got up and sat down on the side of the bed. By this time they were way down the hall, next to the bedroom.

The young man began to try to cast the Devil out of this girl, and she began to fight him and slug him. He worked with her for a while until he gave out, and then I took over. She tried to fight me, and I had to throw her to the floor and sit down on top of her—and she threw my body up against the wall and my head against the wall. She had enough strength to throw me up in the air, but I held on to her arms and I wouldn't turn loose.

Then she wore me out and I rested for a while, and he took over again. She wore him out, then I took over again —because you see, as Jesus says in chapter 12, verses

56

43-45 of the Book of Matthew, "When the unclean spirit is gone out of a man . . . " then that unclean spirit says to himself, "I will return into my house from whence I came out; and when he is come, he findeth it empty, swept, and garnished. Then goeth he, and taketh with himself seven other spirits more wicked than himself, and they enter in and dwell there: and the last state of that man is worse than the first. Even so shall it be also unto this wicked generation." Notice, they enter in and dwell there —*seven other spirits, more wicked than himself.*

"The last state of that man is worse than the first." I had wrestled with this girl about a week before this in the hallway of the church, and she was not this strong. It seemed that she had gained about seven times her strength, and it was all I could do to hold on to her arms as she would throw my body up against the wall. She was sixteen years of age and weighed about 110 pounds, but she had supernatural strength.

I don't believe in giving up so easily. I believe that God's power is stronger than the Devil's power. But now we were fighting *eight* unclean spirits instead of one—because, the Bible says "Then goeth he, and taketh with himself seven other spirits" (that is, seven spirits other than himself, more wicked than himself) and they all of them "enter in and dwell there: and the last state of that man is worse than the first." And if Jesus said it, that is the way it is, regardless of what you think about it. When Jesus says something, that is the way it is.

You can read that Scripture for yourself—because, you see, you have to read Scriptures and study them to see what is going on. You don't reason things out from the natural standpoint—because, you see, the natural man understandeth not the things of God, and neither can he know them. So unless you are in the Bible and willing to obey the Scriptures, you don't know anything about it.

The Devil doesn't mind your being religious; he just doesn't want you to obey the Scriptures. But the Bible says that He that is in me is greater than he that is in the world (*see* 1 John 4:4). That includes the original unclean spirit with his seven friends all combined together—but the One that is within me is greater than he that is in the world. And so we were finally standing there.

We wore the Devil out. She was finally standing against the wall, just staring, and looking at us, and I turned away and walked a few steps and said, "Thank you, Jesus, for your mighty power."

And I walked back over to her, and with as loud a voice as I could, screamed out. I reached way down on the inside of me and got all the breath in me that I could muster up, and I walked up in front of her and I screamed out loud at her: "In the name of Jesus Christ of Nazareth, I command this girl's body to be free from the Devil's power—and I demand in Jesus' name that all of you come out of this girl."

Immediately, her body wilted to the floor, like a lettuce leaf out of the sunshine; and the last state of that girl began crying and weeping, and the joy of the Lord began to come to her, and she wept and wept and wept.

She got in the car in my driveway and they started to take her home. She called me over to the passenger side of the front seat, where she was sitting. She looked at me with the love of God all over her, and she said to me, "I remember what the second thing was that I brought to you." And she reached into her back pocket and took out the double-edged razor blade and handed it to me and said, "Thank God I won't need this now. And thank you, Jesus, for setting me free. And thank you, Mr. Hayes, for being so kind as to scream at me again. Now I can love everybody—because Jesus has accepted me back, and the power of darkness has left me."

And I said to her as I say to everyone, "Now you can stay free, if you will resist the Devil. But you must resist him in Jesus' name; if you will do this, he will flee from you. Just go, young lady, and tell the people the great things the Lord hath done for thee—because, you see, God's church has the same power on earth that it has in heaven."

Jesus wants us to understand that the power from God that He ministered through on the earth, He gave and dedicated over to the church when He went back to heaven. The church is supposed to be operating under the power of God on the earth today, and the New Testament says of those who deny the power of God, they are an abomination in His sight. (*see* Luke 16:15.)

Jesus makes the statement in chapter 22 of the Book of Matthew, verse 29: "Ye do err, not knowing the scriptures, nor the power of God."

Down in verse 32 of that same chapter Jesus says, "I am the God of Abraham, and the God of Isaac, and the God of Jacob. . . . God is not the God of the dead, but of the living." And this sixteen-year-old girl was living, and Jesus loved her, and He wanted her set free from the power of darkness.

And He wants *you* set free from the darkness and the evil spirits and the unclean spirits that drive you away from Him. He wants you to be free from them. And you can be free and stay free in Jesus' name, if you will give Him your life and become a part of the church.

Jesus says in the Book of Matthew, chapter 16 verses 18 and 19, "And I say also unto thee, That thou art Peter, and upon this rock I will build my church; and the gates of hell shall not prevail against it. And I will give unto thee the keys of the kingdom of heaven: and whatsoever thou shalt bind on earth shall be bound in heaven: and whatsover thou shalt loose on earth, shall be loosed in heaven."

You see, the great commission of the Lord Jesus Christ for the church today is in chapter 16 of the Book of Mark: "Go ye into all the world, and preach the gospel to every creature. He that believeth and is baptized shall be saved; but he that believeth not shall be damned. And these signs shall follow them that believe; In my name shall they cast out devils. . . . "

That is the first commission for any believer of the Gospel—"*Commission*. Actually, your first *duty* when you become a child of God is to not be ashamed, to bow down to Him and worship Him and let Him be your God, for He wants us to be His people. "Thou shalt love the Lord thy God with all thine heart, mind, soul, and body." God doesn't want you to have any gods before Him. "Thou shalt love thy neighbor as thyself."

Jesus said, "These are the two great commandments." This sixteen-year-old girl was my neighbor. If I am going to be a part of the church, Jesus would not have been pleased with me had I turned her away or let the Devil win. Because, you see, the Devil is not stronger than Jesus. Jesus lives inside you through the power of the Holy Spirit. "Greater is He that is in you than he that is in the world."

6

The Hippie Cult Leader

Sometime ago in Chattanooga, Tenneessee, Dr. Lester Sumrall and I were working together in a meeting—a three-day meeting sponsored by the Full Gospel Business-men in the YMCA building close to the bypass that goes around Chattanooga. At a morning service—the service was just about over, and we were fixing to close the meet-ing—Dr. Sumrall and I were standing at the altar together, and a young man began to approach the altar, walking up the aisle, and he looked like he came from another world.

He had long hair, a long beard, a sleeveless shirt, tight jeans, Indian moccasins, a leather headband, a long neck-lace around his neck. Tattoos covered his arms, and a black bag was tied around each wrist and hanging down.

As he approached us, I remembered, he said, "Some-thing is playing tricks on my mind. Something has been talking to my mind, and it told me to come in here, and told me to come up to the front."

We just gently reached our hands out to him with a welcome and said, "All right, just let us pray for you." And we immediately made our approach directly to him and took him by the hands gently, and said in no uncertain terms, "Now, Satan, in Jesus' name we command you to come out of him."

And the moment we said that, he broke and began to cry. He was just sobbing. He was crying just like he'd lost

61

his best friend. He kept on crying and crying and crying. Finally, when he could get some words out he said, "God, I didn't know that You loved me."

He kept on crying and saying, "God, I didn't know that You loved me." He kept this up for about thirty minutes, and after about thirty minutes, he said, "You-all, I didn't know that you loved me."

I finally got a chance to talk to him, and the power of God was all over him. He looked so gentle, like a little lamb. He looked at me and said, "I didn't know that God loved me. I didn't even know that God existed and was real."

I said, "Where did you come from?"

He said, "I run a hippie house in Nashville, Tennessee. Me and another boy were on our way to Florida to get a load of acid to take back to the hippie house to sell—and our car broke down out here on the bypass, and my friend wired home for some money to get the car fixed. We were just waiting for the car to get fixed and go on to Florida."

I said, "Well, thank God that trip was cancelled."

And he said, "That's right. I'm not going to Florida to buy acid to take back to feed to the young people."

I asked, "Have you been on dope very long yourself?" He said he had been using it for several years.

I asked, "Didn't you ever realize in your life that God was real?" And he said no.

He looked like he was about twenty-three years of age. I asked him how old he was. He said thirty-two. He looked like Charles Manson's twin brother—about the same size, same hair, and same beard.

"Not one time in my life," he said, "did anyone tell me that God was real, or loved me personally. I had no idea that God loved me. I have been in the penitentiary twice. I used to go across the country robbing places as I would come to them to buy dope, but I never realized that God loved me. I was always motivated by a driving force that wanted me to do what I wanted to do."

I said, "Well, thank God you are free now."

His friend was outside. We went outside in the lobby, and he sat down in the seat. And he kept crying and weeping before the Lord, and his friend kept saying to him all afternoon, "Come on, let's go to Florida. The car will be fixed soon."

He said, "I'm not going. I'm not going."

His friend said, "You are crazy; there is nothing to this. There is nothing to it."

He would look up at his friend and say, "I didn't know God loved me. I didn't know God loved me."

His friend would say, "What about the people in the house in Nashville? What about the load of acid we are supposed to pick up in Florida? Come on, we got to hurry up and leave. . . . " And he would just look up at him, tears running down his face, and say, "But you don't understand. I found out that God loves me—and I didn't know that God loved me before."

That night, I wanted his friend to stay and go into the service. I remember I went downtown one afternoon to stop into the tailor shop to have a suit made, and before I got to the tailor shop, about 4:30 p.m., I had an urge all of a sudden to turn around and go back to the YMCA building, where we were going to hold the last meeting. I went back to the building quickly, and in one of the rooms a group of young people were sitting there talking. The hippie cult leader who had just had the Devil cast out of him was talking to them, and telling them he had found something that was real to him, that he never knew before that God loved him. And his friend was still trying to tell him there was nothing to that.

I walked in, sat down, and began to listen to him—and his friend kept trying to tell him there was nothing to it. I asked him, "What makes you so hard, young man? Don't you believe that Jesus even exists?"

He said, "No, I don't think there is anything to it."

The friend was also from the hippie house in Nashville. He said, "Are you kidding? I went to Bible school for a year at one time in my life, and I got married and grew a beard and let my hair get long, and my wife was ashamed to go into the supermarket with me. She refused to walk to the supermarket with me to buy groceries. I had to sit out in the car and wait on her." I had to admit that he did look like a mess.

He said, "My wife left me and I started doing my own thing. I do not believe there is anything to religion or anything like that. I went to Bible school for a year and had fellowship in a Baptist Church. If there was any great power there, I couldn't tell it."

I said, "It doesn't make any difference what you believe, because Jesus is real anyway," and he said he would like to know if He is or not.

"Oh," I said, "You would like to know if Jesus is real?"

He said, "That is right. I went to Bible school and fooled around with church and I'm getting tired of this stuff. If Jesus is really real, I would like to know it. I would really like you to show me."

I said, "Oh, young man, you are going to get it. Anytime you want Jesus to show you that He is real, He will.

Because, you see, the Bible says that those that hunger and thirst after righteousness shall be filled (*see* Matthew 5:6). So just get a little bit more hungry. Just a little bit more hungry, and you are going to get it. Jesus will work you over, but you need to get hungry."

He said, "I would like for you to show me if He is really real. More than anything in the world, if He is really real, I would like to know."

"Well," I said, "you are just about hungry enough then."

He said, "It is away down deep inside me. I would like it to come out, and I would like to know that."

"Well," I said, "you can see a change in your friend from today at noon."

He said, "Yes, this is not like him at all. He doesn't even act like the same. Before he was always so hard and so high-tempered, and would raise a fight over anything. Now he is like a little lamb."

I said, "Yes, Jesus touched him, and now he is free from that driving force of darkness that has been trying to destroy him for many years. He does not have to be destroyed. He or anyone else. All anyone has to do is reach out and say, 'Jesus, help me,' and He will. Young man, He will help you, too. Because He loves you. I promise you, young man, that Jesus will show you He is real."

So after we sat there and talked a while, it came time for the service to start, and the young man just got the money from home to get his car fixed and to pay the bill.

In the evening, I was sitting up front with Dr. Sumrall and in with a group of young people, sitting towards the back, came this young man that didn't believe there was "anything to that"—except that he really wanted Jesus to show him if He was real.

They were all sitting together. We sang a few songs and then they began to take up an offering for the service. And as the offering plate went by—this young man told me later—it was like an unseen hand had got into his pocket.

"The first thing I knew," he said, "I dropped a ten-dollar bill in the offering plate." And the moment he dropped the ten-dollar bill into the offering plate, God hit him, sitting right there right in the middle of the offering. You know, sometimes God just shocks us, and starts a meeting right in the middle of an offering. Because, you see, you are not going to tell God anything. God is going to do things His way.

About that time the hippie cult leader who was just set free at noon raised up and said, "It is my friend, my friend. He is crying. That's my friend."

So we said, "Bring him up here," and he and another boy got on each side of him and led him towards the front — and he was crying so hard by the time he got to the front, we just reached our hands out and began to pray God's blessing upon him. The Lord just keep flooding his innermost being, and he stood on the floor and began to cry and also to thank Jesus for loving him.

About that time a rebel girl who had been fighting with her mother and taking dope jumped up out of her seat, came down front and began to pray, and we commanded the Devil to come out of her in Jesus' name—and she broke and began to cry. And then another one and then another one came. In a few minutes there were some twenty hippies standing up at the altar, crying and weeping before the Lord. We took authority in Jesus' name and commanded the Devil to come out of them.

The glory of God surged in that place, and the grown-ups and the businessmen began to weep and cry, and nobody could get to sleep that night. Oh, what a glorious service that was!

Dr. Lester Sumrall turned to me and said, "Brother Norvel, I've got to leave and go home to South Bend, Indiana. Why don't you continue this meeting? It would be God's will for you to continue it."

I said, "Well, all right." So I announced that we would continue the meeting. So we did for several nights, with God moving mightily each night.

The next day the hippie cult leader began to walk downtown, telling people he hadn't known God loved him. He even went to the police station and told the police and talked with them, because he had spent a lot of time in penitentiaries and jails. He went down and began to testify and witness to the policemen in the police station, still dressed the same way—with the black bags hanging from his arms, the Indian headband, his necklace, and sleeveless shirt—telling the policeman he hadn't known God loved him, tears streaming down his face.

He said, "I found a new life. I didn't know God loved me, but I met those two fellows, named Lester Sumrall and Norvel Hayes, and they cast the Devil out of me. I was a hippie cult leader on my way to Florida to get acid to sell to the hippies. I served two terms in the penitentiary, and I had no earthly idea that God was real. I never knew before that God loved me."

They called the TV station in town, which was so astounded at his testimony that it came and got him and put him on television, put his picture in the paper with a long article. The town really got shook up.

He went on television with tears streaming down his face, saying, "I didn't know God loved me. I was on my way to Florida to get a load of acid to sell to the hippies —and something started to talk to me when the car broke down and had me go up front in this meeting at the YMCA." Right on television he said, "These fellows cast the Devil right out of me."

That so shook up the TV stars that they got together one night and said, "Where is this meeting at?"

He said, "At the YMCA, and it is still going on."

One night I was getting ready to start the meeting and there came walking in three TV stars.

"We met this hippie cult leader on television," one of them said, "and he said that you fellows had cast the Devil out of him."

I said, "That's right. And now the Lord Jesus Christ has come into his heart and he has found a new life, and it is exciting to him."

They said, "We never heard of anything like this, so we came tonight to see what is going on."

I said, "Well, sit up front in these three seats and you are going to see it again tonight. We will sing a few praise songs unto God, and we will praise the name of Jesus for a while, and will have some prayers, and we will take up a little offering to pay for the expenses of the meeting. Then we are going to have a young fellow speak and several young people to give their testimonies and give an invitation, and you will see God's mighty power moving here tonight. It is very simple. Just don't make God complicated."

So that is what we did, trying to be led by the Spirit of God. I looked over in a little while and one of the TV stars had already broken and was beginning to weep and cry. I just said, "Thank You, Jesus. This service is Yours; do what You want to do."

One of the hippies who got saved was cross-eyed, and he wore real dark thick glasses. His eyes were in terrible shape, and for a few short seconds that night it was like a wave of wind had come through that room. I don't think it lasted over fifteen or twenty seconds—real unusual— and as it came over us that night, diseases began to disappear out of the bodies; and the hippie with the crossed eyes was sitting in front of me, and his eyes just straightened up like an unseen hand had reached down and got him and straightened his eyes up.

As he broke under that power, he took his glasses off, and his eyes were completely straightened, and he had perfect vision. God's mighty healing power—the gift to the church that is mentioned in chapter 12 of 1 Corinthians.

Gifts of healing came to us that night for a few seconds, and then were gone—but, oh, the mighty beautiful work that God's healing power did when it passed through that room! That was a night I shall never forget.

Then the hippie cult leader began to give his testimony of what Jesus meant to him, and the television men began to bring their cameras and take pictures of the meeting for the news on television of what was happening in Chattanooga, Tennessee. And it was beautiful to see the changes in young people's lives that had been warped and detoured in the world of darkness and the power of the Devil, to see that power broken in the name of Jesus by commanding Satan to come out of them.

How easy it was for God to set them free, when we were

not ashamed to obey the Gospel and obey the command that Jesus has given to us as believers—the command in the Book of Mark, sixteenth chapter and seventeenth verse: "In my name shall they cast out devils. . . ."

And you can cast out devils too, if you believe it. Do it with authority and you can see people set free by the multitudes, if they are willing to come for help—because I promise you that, whatever condition you are in, if you will just come to Jesus, seeking help, He will not turn you away.

7

The College Boy Who Lost His Mind

One afternoon, late, I was riding in my car through the shopping center in Cleveland, Tennessee, and all of a sudden the Word of the Lord came unto me, saying, "Go to Chattanooga, Tennessee, now—to the youth center."

Well, I had been at the youth center before, but not for quite some time. So I immediately began to drive towards Chattanooga. I had no idea of what for, but I knew that the Lord wanted me to go.

As I pulled into the driveway to the youth center, the young man who had been a hippie cult leader from Nashville saw my car coming up the driveway, and came running out of the house down through the yard real fast, and he stopped me as I began to park. He said, "Norvel, Norvel, the Lord sent you here—Jesus sent you here."

I said, "Yes, I know He did. What's wrong?"

He said, "There's a college boy upstairs, locked in his room, who has lost his mind, and the Christian psychologist of the college got permission to bring him over here. I want you to meet him."

I said, "Well, all right." So I went in.

"I am Dr. N—," the college psychologist said. "One of our students here lost his mind—a padded-cell case. He would have to have somebody stand guard over him. We can't let him out of the room. He takes his clothes off and goes out in the street and marches with people in the nude."

And he added, "I didn't believe in this sort of thing a year ago, but I had been listening to some tapes by Derek Prince and then I met this young man that was a hippie cult leader, and he said that you and Dr. Lester Sumrall had cast the Devil out of him."

I said, "That's right."

He said, "I could see that he was a completely changed man from somebody who had been on dope and sold dope."

I said, "Oh, yes, he has the love of God in him now, and he can keep it in there if he wants it. You see, you can be a Christian if you want to be one. You don't have to be one, but you can be one if you want to be one. All you have to do is to begin to seek God sincerely. God said that those people that diligently seek Him shall find Him—but many people in darkness don't know how to seek Him, and that is where other Christians come in.

"We are supposed to use the name of Jesus and break the power of the Devil over people's lives when we get a chance, and command Satan to come out of them. God wants the human race to follow Him, not the Devil. All we did was cast the devil out of him."

The psychologist said, "Yes, I can see that. That is the very reason why I got permission to get this young man out of school. You understand that he is in my custody. He is upstairs in one of the rooms. I've got one of his buddies there in the room with him, standing guard over him."

I said, "Well, if he is under your custody, then you will have to make the decision if you want me to pray for him."

"Well," he said, "I do want you to pray for him. A year ago I didn't believe in this sort of thing, but being a Christian psychologist at a college with several hundred students, I am beginning to believe it—to see how real the Devil is."

"Oh, yes," I said, "the Devil is very much alive and he has a lot of power. But he doesn't have as much power as Jesus has. The name of Jesus is all power in heaven and on earth, and I will be glad to pray for him if you want me to. But you are going to have to leave us alone. I don't want a bunch of doubters in the room."

So I walked with the psychologist upstairs and we walked into the room, and there were two college students in the room. One was sitting down and the other one was standing up beside him. They introduced me to the one standing up. We shook hands, and he introduced me to the one sitting down—and he just looked at me and made a funny noise. He didn't even know his own name. He had lost his mind several days before and had had to have guards over him ever since. So as he sat there, I just approached him very gently, and I put the palm of my right hand upon his forehead. And as I laid my hands on the man, I broke the power of Satan over his life:

"Satan, I break and bind thee way down deep inside him, and I command you to obey me. I command you in Jesus' name to turn him loose, and I command you in Jesus' name to turn his mind loose, and for his mind to be restored to normal. And I pray, down inside of him, in the name of the Lord Jesus Christ. I command you to come out of him and let him go free. I say, in Jesus' name your power is broken; and I say come out of him, and I bind your power up in Jesus' name. And I am telling you that you can't destroy him—because I say you can't, and I am not going to let you destroy him. You can't have this

73

young man's mind, because I have been sent here by the Lord Jesus Christ to cast you out, and in Jesus' name I command you to obey me. Come out of him."

I was taking authority over the Devil and letting the Devil know that he had no right to this young man, that I didn't come to play games and I didn't come to ask him anything. I came to cast him out and did not expect anything less; I gave the Devil no choice.

Let me stop here and make a statement to you: You don't give the Devil any choice. You don't *ask* him anything. He had already lost his right. He has already been thrown out of heaven and he is mad about it, so you don't ask him anything. You *tell* him what you want him to do, and you command him to obey you—and unless you waiver in your believing, Satan himself has no choice. He had to flee.

But it has to be done scripturally. Not according to what you think about it. It doesn't make any difference what you think, or what I think, about the Bible. It is what the Bible actually says that is the only thing that will help you—and Jesus says, "In my name, shall they cast out devils." And he doesn't mean for you to ever stop. That doesn't mean just for a while and then you stop.

So after some five minutes of taking authority over the Devil and letting him know who had sent me, I demanded that the young man's mind be restored to normal. I reminded the Devil that his power was broken and he could not stay in this young man's body—that he didn't even have a choice, because I wasn't giving him one, so he had to come out.

I just sat down on a chair several feet from him, and every few minutes I would just say with my mouth, with authority, "In Jesus' name, I said, come out of him. You have no choice, you know. In Jesus' name, come out." And I sat there for another ten minutes and said, "In Jesus' name, come on out."

After maybe some forty-five minutes or an hour, the young man got up from his sitting position, walked over to the opposite corner of the room from where I was sitting, and lay down on the floor, just like a dog, and began to bark like one, and began to say in a real funny voice, "Water, water, I want water. Water, water. I want water. Water, water." So the psychologist went and got him some water and gave it to him.

I could see that they were yielding to the Devil and disturbing my prayer, so I walked over and told them, "Men, I know that you mean well and want this boy's mind restored to him, but you must leave me alone. I may be here for a long time. I am not God, you know. All I do is obey. Jesus said that those that believe in His name shall cast out devils, and that is what I do in Jesus' name; I cast them out and leave the results to Him. Jesus doesn't want him in this state, and that is why Jesus sent me down here. Feeling sorry in the natural standpoint for him is not good enough. He has to have some help, and there is no natural help to help him. The boy has lost his mind. He doesn't even know his own name. Several days ago he was a nice young intelligent boy. Where is he from?"

They said, "He is from New Jersey. His father has been called and is on his way to the college, driving from New Jersey to Chattanooga to pick him up or to make a decision on what he is going to do with him."

Dr. N———said to me, "That is the reason I got permission to get him out of the college and bring him over here where this hippie cult leader was, because he said you fellows cast the Devil out of him, and I thought maybe you could pray for this boy and help him."

I said, "Well, Jesus has worked it out. He spoke to me in my car in Cleveland, Tennessee, and told me to come to Chattanooga. Jesus knew that he was down here, and He wanted me to minister to him. I don't want to fail Jesus, and I don't want to fail this boy—but you fellows have too much unbelief, so I am asking you to leave me alone and let me pray for him if you want him to receive help. If you want to do anything, just believe, in Jesus' name. God is able to restore this boy's mind to him, so join your faith with mine. As I minister to him, agree and believe with me."

So they agreed. For the next four hours, I would just say every few minutes, "In Jesus' name, come out of him." I was sitting down in a chair in the same room with him, and I was very calm. I don't let devils make me nervous, and I don't allow devils to rob me of the peace of God— because, you see, any man that doesn't think straight is a man that doesn't study the Bible, or really doesn't obey or believe what he reads.

God meant what He said in the Bible, and He means what He says, and all we have to do is obey that. He said, "I will go with you"—confirming the Word with signs following—and I would not accept anything except his right mind be restored to him; I was not here to play Gospel games. I was here because Jesus had sent me here, and God would not be pleased with anything except New Testament results—and that meant restoring his right mind to him, and I expected nothing less than that.

So every few minutes I would just merely state, "In

Jesus' name, come out of him. You can't stay in him, because I say you can't. You have to turn his mind loose, because I say you do. His body and his mind will be restored to normal, because I say they will. And I say to you, Satan, you have no choice—so in the name of Jesus, come out of him." For some four hours I did that. Then we decided to take him downstairs.

We took him downstairs to another large room and sat him down in a chair. But when we started to take him down the stiars, at the top of the stairs his body turned real stiff. He would not move his legs to walk down the stairs. We just picked him up and carried him downstairs, just like a statue. We got him down there, and got him to sit down. They even fixed me something to eat, and I ate very calmly. And while I was eating, I kept on saying, "You don't have any choice, Satan. You have to come out. In Jesus' name, I command you to come out of him."

This went on for some two more hours. I was sitting in the chair. He got up out of his seat, walked over in front of me, raised up one leg, stood on one foot, put his other leg back in the air and bent over about a third of the way to the floor, sticking one arm straight out in front of him and the other arm back. He stood on one foot in that position, and as far as I could see he never did move. He just stood there on one foot.

But you see it doesn't make any difference to me what the Devil does. It doesn't shake me up. I just kept saying every ten or fifteen minutes, "In Jesus' name, come out of him." And I said it with authority. I said, "Satan, I am still telling you that you don't have any choice. You can't stay in him, you have to come out."

In a little while, his mouth began to open, and I guess

his mouth opened about an inch—and very slowly I saw his tongue come sliding out of his mouth, very slowly. And his tongue came out some two to three inches. He was still standing on one foot in the strange position.

Some other people were watching by this time and I told them to be very quiet. I asked them, "Did you ever see a demon come out of a person?"

They said, "No. No, we never have."

I said, "Well, watch here and you'll see something you never saw before."

At the side of his mouth, white foam and saliva began to ooze out very slowly—and then more often I would say, "In Jesus' name, come on out." In another minute or two, I would say it again, "In Jesus' name, I said, come on out."

This white foam and salvia began to flow and run down on the floor from his mouth, little puddles of it forming on the floor. After a while no more came out. He was still standing on one foot.

I said, "Now let us pick him up and put him in bed." You know, his body would not come back normally. We put him in bed like that, really stiff. We just had to lay him in a position and force his arms back to a normal position.

I said, "All right—Jesus said in Mark 11:23 that one who believes can have 'whatsoever he saith.' Jesus said also in Mark 11:24, 'What things soever ye desire, when ye pray, believe that ye receive them, and ye shall have them.'

"Now I am going to lay my hands on his head, and I am going to ask his right mind be restored to him as he sleeps the rest of the night. I want you to agree with me that as he sleeps the mighty power of God will restore his mind completely. The Devil has no power over him anymore to keep his mind." And they agreed.

The next morning they called me at home. They said, "This fellow is in bed with his tongue hanging out and looks about half dead."

I said, "Well, he is not—the Devil doesn't have any choice; he has to turn him loose, he has to come out of him."

The men said to me, "They want you to come down here. His father is on his way, and he will be here this morning."

I said, "Well, I will be down there after a while."

In about five minutes my phone rang again. They told me they had gone in and looked at him again " . . . and he looks terrible. His tongue is hanging out."

I said, "I'm telling you, the Devil does not have any choice; he must come out. And his mind will be restored to normal. Now you believe me. It has already been spoken, and that is the way it is. So I will come down there real quick."

I got in my car and began to drive to Chattanooga, saying, "Devil, you can't keep this man; your power has been broken, and you know it has been broken. You are not going to destroy his mind. I am not going to let you.

"In Jesus' name I command his mind to be restored to normal, in Jesus' name. I plead the blood of Jesus over this young man. The blood of Jesus was shed on the Cross for our salvation, and for him to be free. Jesus came to set the captives free. I won't accept anything less than freedom for this young man."

Some fifteen to twenty minutes later I pulled up in the driveway, entered the center and walked to the door of the living room. There were a lot of people in the living room, and this young man was sitting in the living room carrying on a normal conversation. He jumped up out of his seat and said with his mouth, "I have never seen him before in my life."

He started to run over towards me and put his arms around me, and began to thank me for coming and praying for him—and talked just as normally as anybody.

He was carrying on a conversation with us just as normally as anyone. He knew his own name. He knew the other people. In a few minutes, his father from New Jersey walked in. They said they wanted me to talk to his father.

I said, "Mister, I need to talk to you for a while. I need to ask you some questions. The first question I want to ask you is, what kind of church do you go to in New Jersey?"

He said "Well, I go to a Bible-believing church."

And I said to him, "Well, they all believe that, but that is not good enough. There is a difference between saying you believe the Bible with your head and obeying the Scriptures in action. Sir, do you go to a New Testament church? One that believes that Jesus Christ came into the world to set captives free? Do you go to a church that is not ashamed of the Gospel of the Lord Jesus Christ? Do they call people down front and lay hands on them and have God's power surge through them? Do they anoint people with oil and pray for the sick where you go to church? Do they cast out devils in Jesus' name where you go to church?"

He said, "No, I do not think my pastor knows anything about that."

"Well, sir," I said, "I am going to tell you something. You don't have just a normal case on your hands. The

Devil has come to destroy your son. You know that he has been pulling off his clothes and going out in the streets, marching with people in the nude. The devils have come to destroy him, and they will be watching his house that they came out of. And they will return again, Jesus said. And if they find his house 'empty, swept, and garnished,' they will go and get seven other spirits more wicked than themselves and come back into him and dwell in that house—and he will be in worse shape than he was before. So I am warning you now that you had better take this young man when you get back home and find a church that believes in the New Testament in action, and not just in its head.

"Head knowledge of the Bible doesn't bring God's power, because faith without action is dead. God wants people to *do* something. Not just *believe* something and not do it. God warns us to be doers of the Word and not hearers only, and I am telling you for your own good, and to save you thousands of dollars.

"You had better find a New Testament church where this young man has a right to go to the altar of God and kneel down and begin to worship God, where the pastor will come down and lay his hands on his head and ask God's power to heal him and to fill him. He is going to be full of something, and you had better help him stay full of God—so that when the evil powers from hell return, he will be full of God. That way, they can't get back in. They have no choice but to turn around and leave again—and roam backwards and forth through the air searching and seeking somebody else.

"Your son is your responsibility. Help him find a New Testament church that believes in the delivering and keeping power of God, and keep the presence of God flowing through him. Will you do it?"

He said, "Yes, sir, I will try to find one."

The last word I heard from him was that he had gone back to New Jersey and found an Assembly of God church—and I thought, "Well, most of them know something about it. They will invite you to come to the altar. They should know how to help you."

It wasn't very long until I received a call from the Christian psychologist, Dr. N————and he invited me to come to Chattanooga. He said he and the college president wanted me to have lunch with them at the college.

I went down and had lunch with them. While we were having lunch, the president of the college told me how he appreciated my working with that boy. He had heard what happened, and after lunch he wanted me to go into the office and hold hands and pray for the college, and I said, "Okay, yes sir, I will be glad to do that."

So after lunch we walked to the college office and held hands, and I prayed God's blessing upon that college— because, you see, this young man got his life all fouled up in some goofed-up sex spirits and sex acts, and the Devil had him take his clothes off and march with people in the streets nude.

And I am warning you, young people and college students across America who read this book: This streaking business that is going on across college campuses now . . . you really don't know what you are doing. You are opening up the door to the Devil to possess your body. He will go from your body to your mind, and you will be so mixed-up. If you continue in that mess, you could easily have your mind snap and spend years from home in a mental institution, sitting around for years wondering who you are and not remembering your own name.

God wants you to live for Him from the days of your youth. Don't give your body over to the Devil. Don't get yourself hung up in goofed-up sex acts. Don't let your body get mixed up with streaking on the college campuses. In the last twenty years of my life I have visited nearly every college campus of any size from Boston to Seattle, Washington, and I have seen the different fads come and go. I have seen the different dances come and go. You can get by for a while on certain dances. You can get by for a while on certain things. God's mercy stretched out to us is what pulls us through all of our mistakes.

Don't turn your body over to the Devil. God says in the first chapter of Romans that you had better keep your sex life straight—under the laws of God, in marriage in other words, man with woman and woman with man. And God warns you in that chapter, if you don't do it He will turn you over to a reprobate mind (*see* Romans 1:28). You will wind up with a mind just like a snake's. Never know feelings again. Never a chance to reach God again, because you failed to keep things straight. Be sure you do not fail to keep your sex life in natural affection, as God intended it, man with woman and woman with man.

Young person, don't let a bunch of your friends challenge you to streak and open the door of the Devil's power to come and possess your body, possess your mind. The Lord Jesus Christ has a beautiful life for you, but you must learn—and learn quickly— that you will have to obey Him in order to enjoy that life.

Jesus said, "I have come that ye might have life and have it more abundantly" (*see* John 10:10), and Jesus cast the seven devils out of Mary Magdalene. She followed Him from that day forward. In the act of adultery (*see* John 8:3-11), Jesus told the people, "Let him without sin among you cast the first stone," and they all left; and Jesus raised up after writing in the sand, with no one there except Him and the woman, and said, "Where are thine accusers?" She said, "No man condemns me." And He said, "Neither do I. Thy sins be forgiven thee. Go and sin no more."

So, young people, I advise you to spend time praying. And college students, I know that it is very important to you to get a college education and a degree, but I can tell you something that will be more valuable to your life than any college degree from any university in America. The greatest thing for your life is to learn how to pray—greater than to get a college degree. A college degree is fine. But if you could get that degree *plus* learning how to pray, you could be a giant for God. Learn while you are young how to pray, and learn about the compassion of the Lord Jesus Christ, and how in Jesus' name to cast out devils.

8

The Doctor's Wife Who Cut Her Wrists

I was visiting one of my restaurants one Sunday afternoon and one of my employees came and told me, "Telephone, Mr. Hayes." I went to the telephone and the voice on the other end was that of a lady I had worked with and prayed with, who had been dying. I had prayed and broken the power of the Devil over her life, and she was such a blessing to me for a long time after that, and she still is.

She said, "Norvel, Norvel, there is a doctor's wife in another city who is desperate. She has cut her wrists and tried to kill herself, and they can't find anybody to go and minister to her and help her, but I told them you would if I could find you. I have been trying to find you all afternoon. Would you go with me and minister to this woman if my husband and I take you?"

They came down and I got in their car and we drove to the city. We had a hard time finding the house, as we had never been there before. It seemed as though the Devil was trying to keep us away from the house, but finally we found it.

We walked in; and out of the bedroom, in a housecoat, came a beautiful young lady about twenty-eight years of age.

She said, "My life is so messed up. I am a doctor's wife,

and I have been taking some pills. I found out my husband was going with another woman. I just didn't think there was anything else to live for."

I said, "Young lady, there is a lot to live for. Just because he wants to go the ways of the Devil there is no sign you have to destroy yourself. What did you cut your wrists for?"

She said, "Something has been trying to get me to cut my wrists for four years."

So I kept talking to her. She said, "My father killed himself out here behind the house, in the woods. I guess our lives have been so messed up, so many heartaches."

I said, "Yes, the Devil has been around here, but I came here today to run him off. You see, young lady, that suicide demon that kept trying to tempt your father, that lived in him and tried to tell him to kill himself, he finally got the job done. Your father took his last breath out in those woods, and when he died that demon came out of him—and he is still roaming around here on these grounds. He thinks he owns this place, and he is trying to do his damage against you. He talked your father into it, and he is going to try to talk you into it; but I came today in Jesus' name to break his power. You are not ever going to kill yourself. Do you understand me? I am going to pray for you now."

I reached out and laid my hands on her head and said, "You foul suicide spirit, in Jesus' name I command you to come out of this woman."

The moment I said that she broke and began to cry, and fell on the floor on her knees just weeping and crying like she had been shot with a gun.

I said, "This woman's body is free from you and is going

to be filled up with God today, and she is going to go to church and serve the Lord Jesus Christ. And I began to go through every room in the house, praying, and telling the suicide demon that he had no right in that house whatsoever, and in Jesus' name to get out, and in Jesus' name to stay out.

I said, "This girl belongs to Jesus now, and she is going to serve Him. He died on the Cross for her, and the blood of Jesus is on this house because I plead the blood of Jesus over every room of this house and over this property. Get yourself off this property, and get off now, in the name of the Lord Jesus Christ. And I plead the blood of Jesus on this property that you will never do any more damage. This girl is not going to listen to you anymore. You are not going to kill this girl, because I am not going to let you kill her."

She said, "Thank God" in her tears. "Thank God, thank God. He has been trying to make me kill myself for four years, ever since my daddy killed himself out there in the woods behind the house."

And I said now, "Young lady, do you go to church anyplace?"

"Well," she said, "I hardly ever go."

I said, "You are going to start. You have to get yourself identified with the body of Christ. You have to take part in the church of the Lord Jesus Christ. You have to serve Him, work for Him, give your money to Him. And you have to show Jesus that you mean business and that you love Him—and that all the suicide demons in the world can't talk you into anything. Don't worry, you are a free woman."

She said, "Yes, yes, I know I am. I never felt like this

before. I'm free. I'm free. He has no power over me."

I said, "That right. And I want you to be filled with God, and God's power will take you right through every storm and every darkness that tries to come upon your life. In Jesus' name, you are free. In Jesus' name you can stay free. But you must serve Him. You go to church and get involved in God's work. Bow down before Him and spend time worshiping Him. Your answer, then, is in Jesus Christ—not anyplace else.

"Jesus said, 'Those that diligently seek Me shall find Me.' So seek Him on your own and find Him for yourself. Take His hand and march with Him—from Matthew through the Book of Revelation—and you will find out just what kind of Jesus He is. He came to give you life and give it more abundantly." So we left the house.

I checked up on her after that and talked to her. I said, "Are you going to church?"

She said, "Yes, my life has changed completely."

I said, "Sure it has changed; Jesus loves you and He wants you to serve Him. You were made to serve Him." And she thanked me for coming and taking authority over that suicide demon and casting that thing out of her. Because, you see, the first duty of the believer, Jesus said, is "in My name shall they cast out devils."

"Young lady," I said to her, "now that you have Jesus in you through the power of the Holy Spirit, you have authority, you have the power to run the Devil off. The next time he tries to come on this property, or bring any temptation on you to commit suicide or to do wrong, shut your fist up just like you were going to fight, and in that moment say with authority, 'I resist you, Satan, in Jesus' name, and I command you to get out of this house, and off this property. And get away from me now, because I love the Lord my God with all my heart, all my soul, with all my mind, all the days that I shall live. And Him only will I serve.' "

When you do this, you will find that the Devil will leave you; and the sweet angels of the Lord will come to you, just as they came to Jesus at the end of His forty days and nights on the mountain. And, oh—how sweet it is to live in Jesus. Glory be to God forevermore.

Norvel Hayes shares God's Word boldly and simply, with an enthusiasm that captures the heart of the hearer. He has learned through personal experience that God's Word can be effective in every area of life and that it will work for anyone who will believe it and apply it.

Norvel owns several businesses which function successfully despite the fact that he spends over half his time away from the office, ministering the Gospel throughout the country. His obedience to God and his willingness to share his faith have taken him to a variety of places. He ministers in churches, seminars, conventions, colleges, prisons — anywhere the Spirit of God leads.

For a complete list of tapes and books
by Norvel Hayes, write:
Norvel Hayes
P. O. Box 1379
Cleveland, TN 37311
*Feel free to include your prayer requests and comments
when you write.*